Draw & Write Children's Journal

Speedy Publishing, LLC
40 E Main Street
Newark, Delaware19711
Contact Us: 1-888-248-4521

Website: http://www.speedypublishing.com

DRAW A PICURE OF TODAY'S DISCOVERY

DRAW A PICURE OF TODAY'S DISCOVERY

DRAW A PICURE OF TODAY'S DISCOVERY

DRAW A PICURE OF TODAY'S DISCOVERY

DRAW A PICURE OF TODAY'S DISCOVERY

DRAW A PICURE OF TODAY'S DISCOVERY

DRAW A PICURE OF TODAY'S DISCOVERY

DRAW A PICURE OF TODAY'S DISCOVERY

DRAW A PICURE OF TODAY'S DISCOVERY

DRAW A PICURE OF TODAY'S DISCOVERY

DRAW A PICURE OF TODAY'S DISCOVERY

DRAW A PICURE OF TODAY'S DISCOVERY

DRAW A PICURE OF TODAY'S DISCOVERY

DRAW A PICURE OF TODAY'S DISCOVERY

DRAW A PICURE OF TODAY'S DISCOVERY

DRAW A PICURE OF TODAY'S DISCOVERY

DRAW A PICURE OF TODAY'S DISCOVERY

DRAW A PICURE OF TODAY'S DISCOVERY

DRAW A PICURE OF TODAY'S DISCOVERY

DRAW A PICURE OF TODAY'S DISCOVERY

DRAW A PICURE OF TODAY'S DISCOVERY

DRAW A PICURE OF TODAY'S DISCOVERY

DRAW A PICURE OF TODAY'S DISCOVERY

DRAW A PICURE OF TODAY'S DISCOVERY

DRAW A PICURE OF TODAY'S DISCOVERY

DRAW A PICURE OF TODAY'S DISCOVERY

DRAW A PICURE OF TODAY'S DISCOVERY

DRAW A PICURE OF TODAY'S DISCOVERY

DRAW A PICURE OF TODAY'S DISCOVERY

DRAW A PICURE OF TODAY'S DISCOVERY

DRAW A PICURE OF TODAY'S DISCOVERY

DRAW A PICURE OF TODAY'S DISCOVERY

DRAW A PICURE OF TODAY'S DISCOVERY

DRAW A PICURE OF TODAY'S DISCOVERY

DRAW A PICURE OF TODAY'S DISCOVERY

DRAW A PICURE OF TODAY'S DISCOVERY

DRAW A PICURE OF TODAY'S DISCOVERY

DRAW A PICURE OF TODAY'S DISCOVERY

DRAW A PICURE OF TODAY'S DISCOVERY

DRAW A PICURE OF TODAY'S DISCOVERY

DRAW A PICURE OF TODAY'S DISCOVERY

DRAW A PICURE OF TODAY'S DISCOVERY

DRAW A PICURE OF TODAY'S DISCOVERY

DRAW A PICURE OF TODAY'S DISCOVERY

DRAW A PICURE OF TODAY'S DISCOVERY

DRAW A PICTURE OF TODAY'S DISCOVERY

DRAW A PICURE OF TODAY'S DISCOVERY

DRAW A PICURE OF TODAY'S DISCOVERY

CPSIA information can be obtained
at www.ICGtesting.com
Printed in the USA
BVHW012146080720
583305BV00007B/110

9 781633 835269